Hold On Tight

A Collection of Verse

by

John Wallbridge

Grosvenor House
Publishing Limited

John Wallbridge is hereby identified as author of this
work in accordance with Section 77 of the Copyright, Designs
and Patents Act 1988

The book cover picture is copyright to Lara Allport

This book is published by
Grosvenor House Publishing Ltd
28-30 High Street, Guildford, Surrey, GU1 3HY.
www.grosvenorhousepublishing.co.uk

A CIP record for this book
is available from the British Library

ISBN 978-1-906645-54-0

Contents

CONTENTS

CONTENTS

Cover artwork by Lara Allport
www.thenationalgrid.com.au

Alone

The little old lady who is frail and small
has a family who never see her at all.
She knows it's pointless to grumble or moan -
just sits in her chair, sad and alone.

Each morning she rises and makes her bed,
then reads a book that she's already read.
It's the same routine day after day,
in her own little world with nothing to say.

She was restless and wide awake one night,
thinking nobody cared about her plight.
She decided to end her life of hell,
then hung herself in her prison cell.

1

Bedtime

Her snoring's so loud I can't sleep tonight,
I'm sat up in bed and I've turned on the light -
looked at my alarm clock, it's quarter to three,
and now her bum's blowing raspberries at me.

Her legs thrash about as she starts dreaming,
it's driving me mad, I feel like screaming.
Now she's turned over and is very near,
I finally crack when she burps in my ear.

"I can't take no more", I shout and holler,
drag her off the bed by her collar.
She looks at me sadly and raises her paw,
then gives up and falls asleep on the floor.

2

Blind Date

Sat in a country pub one evening at eight,
was a young man who had a blind date.
His date turned up, so he bought her a drink,
straight away he noticed a terrible stink.

They got on well, both had plenty to say,
spent the evening laughing and chatting away.
As she sat there drinking her lager and lime
the smell was getting worse all the time.

He felt horrible but asked her about the smell.
She said, "Oh my God can you smell it as well?"
Told him her guide dog was still only young,
and had a thing about rolling in horses' dung.

3

Broken Heart

Is there somebody who mends broken hearts?
This one needs rebuilding with many parts.
Gave it to someone who said they'd be true,
but they just used it then tore it in two.

They took the love, told lie after lie,
got hold of the kindness then bled it dry.
Walked over the feelings 'til they wouldn't stay,
destroyed all longing and threw it away.

Abused the trust, inflicted great pain.
Exhausted all passion, extinguished its flame.
In a river of tears the emotion was drowned,
devotion lies shattered all over the ground.

A good looking stranger's now lifted this gloom,
heart's feeling much better, it's going boom-boom.
If they fancy being more than just a friend,
I reckon this broken heart will soon mend.

4

Cash in Hand

I was brought up to know right from wrong;
I'm as honest as the day is long.
Don't steal from others, that would be unkind,
I always hand in whatever I find.

Found a purse in the street one day,
picked it up and was soon on my way.
Thought how upset the owner must be,
gave it to a policeman, who thanked me.

Then I found a wallet on the floor -
it was full of banknotes galore.
Inside was the address of a "Mr Black",
so I found his house and handed it back.

Found a suitcase, it seemed a bit funny,
it was overflowing with lots of money.
But I knew what I had to do -
I bloody well kept it. Well wouldn't you?

Chalk and Rubber

The chalk upset the blackboard rubber,
made him so sad he started to blubber.
Rubber told chalk "Every time you write,
You turn the lovely blackboard white."

Rubber thought chalk was very mean
as he struggled to keep the blackboard clean.
Chalk ignored him, kept writing away,
but gradually got a bit smaller each day.

Blackboard had a word in rubber's ear,
said "Don't fret, you've nothing to fear.
That chalk is acting like a fool,
will soon disappear to nothing at all."

Chalk noticed his writing was getting poor,
told rubber "You won't have to worry much more.
Now I'm so small I won't last long,
a few more words then I'll be gone."

Told the rubber "Once I've gone away
there's a big box of chalks waiting to play."
Rubber winced and said "Oh my lord!"
as the new chalk scribbled all over the board.

6

Choppers

I got all excited when my sister Mary
showed me her pound coin from the tooth fairy.
If what she told me is the truth,
the fairy gives you a pound for each tooth.

Reckon I could be a wealthy young man
with a bit of help from my old Gran.
At bedtime tonight I won't grumble or moan,
as tomorrow I'll have pound coins of my own.

Mum read a story then turned out the light,
pretended I was asleep when Dad said goodnight.
Then I lifted my pillow and placed underneath
thirty- two of those money-making teeth.

Woke up this morning and something's not right;
nothing has happened during the night.
I think the tooth fairy is really cruel,
she's ignored my teeth, left no money at all.

At breakfast Mum told Gran "Don't despair,
I'm sure your false teeth will turn up somewhere."
I'll be in big trouble later today -
I thought they were worthless, so threw them away.

Dented Pride

The other day in the baker's shop
a bloke ran inside, made himself look a clot.
He tripped and fell over, then looked very glum,
everyone had seen him land flat on his bum.

He jumped up quick, then went bright red,
asked for six rolls and a loaf of bread.
The baker said "You've dented my floor",
which caused giggles and laughter galore.

He stood at the counter with a sore hide,
said "It's not dented as much as my pride.
That's the trouble with being a twenty stone copper,
people find it funny when you come a cropper."

8

Double Trouble

Last night's meal has left me unwell,
this morning my stomach's going through hell.
Been sat so long on this toilet seat,
that I've lost all feeling in both my feet.

Few hours ago I was drinking red wine
thinking my curry "looked just fine".
But this morning I'm bent over double,
and my poor bum is clearly in trouble.

Each time I try rising from this toilet pan,
I have to sit back down as fast as I can.
Don't think that I can take much more,
the loo roll's empty and my bum's red raw.

My wife who was showing no sympathy at all
said "I spiked your meal you sad old fool."
Then she shouted, her voice full of hate
"Serves you right for sleeping with my best mate."

End of the Road

I've struggled getting to work this week,
each day my journey's been hard to complete.
At least this nightmare will soon end -
when I get my new car at the weekend.

Caught the bus on Monday, it wasn't great,
it was packed and turned up late.
Complained to the driver, he said "Take a hike",
so the following day I took my bike.

Rode my bike on Tuesday, it's nothing grand,
a real bone - shaker I got second hand.
As I was thinking "this bike's okay",
the wheels fell off and the frame gave way.

Wednesday with a helmet too big for my head,
I rode my son's moped to work instead.
The helmet slipped and I couldn't see,
wrecked the moped when I hit a tree.

Got a lift on Thursday with my mate Geoff,
he drove like a loony and scared me to death.
I decided on Friday to ride on the train,
waited for ages, but it never came.

Picked my car up on Saturday, it's brand new,
drove around all day, the time just flew.
On Sunday morning I turned ghostly white;
someone had nicked it during the night.

10

Equal Shares

One day Robin Hood said to Little John
"I need some advice, my plan has gone wrong.
If I take from the rich to give to the poor,
I have the same problem as I did before.

In theory it's good but there is one hitch,
the rich become poor and the poor become rich."
Little John said "It's simple, each person will gain.
Share the wealth equally, so everyone's the same."

People came to the forest from everywhere,
all of them wanting an equal share.
After the wealth was divided amongst so many,
each person received just half a penny.

Maid Marian told Robin "You silly fool,
they've all ended up with not much at all.
Now you'll be remembered for evermore
as the man who made everybody poor."

Exploding Parade

Filled a bucket with sand, I used my spade,
then put in a firework called Exploding Parade,
the instructions said "Danger, handle with care,
light the fuse then watch as it shoots in the air."

We all stood looking as it coughed and spluttered
"It sounds like it's dying" somebody muttered.
Then all of a sudden it made a loud whoosh,
took off and set light to next doors bush.

Put out the bush fire without too much fuss.
Heard someone say "Look out, it's heading for us!"
Exploding Parade must have wanted to stay,
it turned mid-flight and was coming our way.

People were running and trying to hide,
I watched as it landed, right by my side.
I was thinking it must be finished for sure
when the bugger decided to take off once more.

When it finally exploded it was a delight,
its cascading colours were a beautiful sight.
Now you can't buy them, they're no longer made,
but I'll always remember my Exploding Parade.

12

Family Gatherings

All the family have gathered in their Sunday best,
everyone has decided to dress to impress.
They are here for a christening, the baby looks sweet,
then later there's drinks and something to eat.

At the next get together all of them dress smart;
it's a family wedding, so they must look the part.
They all watch as the bride and groom kneel,
then after it's drinks and a sit down meal.

They have all met up for a funeral today,
show their respect by wearing smart black or grey.
Most of the family are in a sombre mood,
but still end up drinking and eating some food.

At a big family party they had to laugh
when one of the kids said he thought it was daft -
birth, marriage or death why do grown ups think
they must dress smart, then eat and drink?

⟨⟨⟨❧⟩⟩⟩

Fantasy Land

Mum and Dad drink from morning 'til night,
then scream at Lucy "Get out of our sight."
Hides in her bedroom while Dad's deciding
whether to give her another good hiding.

Poor little Lucy was only aged four,
her fragile body could take no more.
She lies on her bed, still and serene,
then drifts off into a beautiful dream.

She dreams of a far away fantasy land
where a flying unicorn takes her hand.
She sits on his back and they soar through the sky,
as marshmallow clouds go sailing on by.

In her fantasy land everything is fine,
people are happy and smile all the time.
There's no such thing as anger or hate,
everybody you meet becomes a good mate.

The unicorn whispered soft in her ear
"Time to wake up we are now here."
Lucy opened her eyes and screamed "Yahoo"
when she realised her dream had come true.

Now every day she's surrounded by love
in her special place way up above.
She is finally free to laugh and play,
forever safe and out of harm's way.

Fresh Vegetables

The fresh healthy veg growing in the ground
wait 'til evening when no one's around.
Then they get drunk on home made punch,
which turns them into a right randy bunch.

Both the broccoli and runner bean
have got the potato very keen.
Cauliflower's a bit of a tease -
Keeps on flirting with the peas.

Brussels sprouts have got it bad,
the sexy swede is driving them mad.
All the parsnips are having a bet
on who gets lucky with the courgette.

The marrow has got a secret wish
to date the asparagus, who is a right dish.
Cabbage reckons it would be fun
to chase the onion and pinch its bum.

Down on their allotment vegetable plot
they really were a saucy lot.
Then a man with a fork came along,
dug them all up and now they are gone.

Great Rarity

In the early hours of the morning
when no one is around,
that's when this great rarity
is most likely to be found.

Should you happen to spot one
it will take you by surprise,
they're so rarely seen nowadays
you won't believe your eyes.

Some people might not trust you -
think you're not telling the truth,
unless you take your camera
so you've got some proof.

If by chance you get lucky,
you'll have every right to gloat
when you hand out the photos
of the milkman and his float.

16

Grim Reaper

He stood on the bridge, looking down at the sea,
thought "At least when I'm dead they'll remember me."
The grim reaper appeared, said "It's not your time,
just listen to me and you will be fine.

It may sound harsh but it needs to be said -
you'll soon be forgotten once you are dead.
Some people may mourn, others will cry,
but the grieving will end and tears soon dry.

You might have a burial or maybe you'll burn,
one gets you a headstone, the other an urn.
The flowers will wilt then they'll be gone,
time quickly passes and people move on.

So come down off that bridge, don't take your life,
return back home to your kids and wife.
Things are never as bad as they seem to be;
it can all be sorted if you avoid me."

The grim reaper thought, "I tried to be kind,
but I couldn't make him change his mind.
He's just jumped and what hurts me the most,
is that I never realised – he's deaf as a post."

Grounded

A little bird's being harassed by a cat.
The bird stays calm, doesn't get in a flap,
watches the cat as he climbs the tree
then spreads his wings and flies away free.

The cat's annoyed he missed his chance
and is now standing on a very thin branch,
watches the bird as he keeps flying around,
then loses his balance and falls to the ground.

The cat looked shocked as he walked away,
Bird got in his tree then sang all day.
Thought to himself "I may only be small
But I made that big cat look a right fool."

Then as soon as the bird turned his back,
cat fired a catapult and said "Take that."
A stone hit the bird right on the head,
as he fell out the tree he was already dead.

18

Guess What I Saw

You'll never guess what I saw today.
It was disgusting, and blew me away.
I looked in amazement at what went on;
now, I'm no prude, but this was all wrong.

It really was an appalling sight -
being committed in broad daylight.
Most people walked by, others just stared,
no one tried to stop it, nobody dared.

What I was seeing was totally insane,
hope I never come across it again.
One taking part was aggressive and mean,
some would say he was being obscene.

They ran off when their task was complete.
I just stood there, white as a sheet.
Are you ready to hear what made me turn pale?
Well you'll have to guess, because I'll never tell.

Hold on Tight

There were three donkeys at the seaside,
who all the children loved to ride.
But one day just for a dare,
the kids took the donkeys to the fair.

On the big dipper, high off the ground,
the donkeys whinnied all the way round.
Rode the waltzer, it gave them a fright,
grabbed each others saddles and held on tight

All posed and acted like big movie stars
as they drove around on the bumper cars.
They decided to have just one more ride -
ended up on the helter skelter slide.

Donkeys thanked the kids, said "Today's been a lark"
then returned to the beach, before it got dark.
Now the donkeys are famous and very well known,
they go to the fair each day on their own.

So if you pay a visit to the seaside
and decide to go on a donkey ride,
keep holding on tightly and be aware,
you just might end up going to the fair.

20

Housing

This tired old house thinks it's a disgrace,
that flats keep appearing all over the place.
Houses round here that people called home
have become flats, so I'm now all alone.

My bricks are crumbling, my roof is leaking,
windows are rotten, floor boards keep creaking.
I've been neglected, I'm derelict and old,
but in my overgrown garden the sign says "Sold".

When my new owners arrive I'm pretty sure
they'll soon have me looking real good once more.
Reckon the flats next door will be impressed,
when they see me done up and at my best.

The builders turned up and before very long
walls are knocked down and bits added on.
A few months later the men with hard hats
have turned me into six one bedroom flats.

21

In Trouble Again

He's tired, lost and feeling sad,
knows his parents will be going mad.
Then Dad runs towards him, looking mean,
cuffs his ear, shouts "Where have you been?"

Told him that Mum's pulling out her hair,
she's been looking for him everywhere.
"For the last hour I've been searching too.
We are both very cross with you."

He said "Sorry Dad if I've been a pain
but I promise not to do it again.
I've been out hunting for some grub
I'm a very hungry young lion cub."

Soon his Dad softened his tone,
gave him a lick and they headed home.
He said tonight son you're in for a feast,
Mum has caught us a large wildebeest.

Jilted

There's an old spooky house at the end of a lane.
Rumour has it, if you enter you don't leave again.
It's supposed to be haunted by a young jilted bride,
who will use all her charms to keep you inside.

They say she has the most beautiful face,
a perfect figure, not a hair out of place.
Golden skin that glistens and sparkling blue eyes,
but as well as her beauty, she is clever and wise.

I called at the old house, I wanted to see
if anyone was there who would talk to me.
I'll admit being cautious as I went through the door,
then shocked and amazed by the sight that I saw.

There was an old lady in a large rocking chair,
with wrinkly dry skin and straggly grey hair.
She turned towards me, then her eyes opened wide,
said "How do you do? I'm the young jilted bride."

I asked her if she had a spare room
for someone who once was a foolish young groom.
She said "I have and it's yours for free,
if tonight you come along haunting with me."

We are getting on well, but must be insane,
have both agreed to give marriage a go once again.
At our wedding the spirits said "Lets have a toast,
all raise your glasses to the bride and groom ghosts."

J.I.Wallbridge

John Ian Wallbridge that's my full name.
I'm the last in line, ain't that a shame.
Was an only child, born in sixty – one,
Always thought I'd have kids, but I've got none.
Looking back I've still enjoyed this life,
Love waking each morning next to my wife.
Been lucky in some ways, I like being me -
Reckon whatever will be will be.
I like to live life at a leisurely pace,
Don't want to be part of the mad rat race.
Got no control over destiny or fate,
Enjoy today, tomorrow may be too late.

King of Hearts

The King of Hearts thought "When my family play,
they all split up and go their own way.
Pontoon, Whist or Snap, I don't know why,
it's chaos no matter what game we try.

Jack, who's the eldest, thinks that it's funny
to go and join Spades when we play Rummy.
Little Ace is no better, he stays well hid,
joins his friend in Diamonds when we play Crib.

Their nine brothers and sisters are the same,
they all disappear whatever the game.
Queen's the worst, thinks she's a Joker,
hanging round Clubs if we play Poker."

The King had an idea that was quite clever -
thought of a game they could all play together.
They all groaned when the King of Hearts said
"Lets have a game of Patience instead."

⸙

Last Waltz

One-two-three and quick-quick-slow
we're giving ballroom dancing a go.
Both late starters, never done it before,
I'm eighty-three and she's eighty-four.

First of all we danced the Foxtrot,
the harder we tried the worse we got.
Next came the Rumba, we weren't much good,
we've got two left feet and legs of wood.

Tried the Tango, she said "Look out, Bert,"
we both fell over then laughed 'til it hurt.
Danced the Waltz in our own special way,
then me and Flo called it a day.

We stopped dancing as the clock struck three,
then sat down for a nice cup of tea.
Both agreed it's too late for us old codgers
to become Fred Astaire and Ginger Rogers.

26

Let's Go Round Again

Jimmy stood, all excited, by his Dad's side,
it's his first ever time on a fairground ride.
Dad told him "Don't worry, this rides no big deal,"
as they queued to go on the ferris wheel.

Jimmy sat in his seat as the ride went round,
then said "Look Dad, we're high off the ground."
Much to his surprise he's not scared at all,
he's having a great time and thinks this ride's cool.

Dad thought this ride was a good idea,
but now he's not sure and is shaking with fear.
He tries to act tough, puts on a brave face,
hoping that he's not sick all over the place.

Jimmy wished they could stay on this ride all night.
Dad's white as a sheet and holding on tight.
When their time was up he heard Jimmy complain,
then say "Come on Dad, let's go round again."

Losing Weight

January and February I went to the gym,
got hot and sweaty but never got slim.
Doesn't matter how much I exercise -
my bum and tum wobble and so do my thighs.

March and April I swam every day,
but this extra weight will not go away.
When I did a dive I made such a wave -
nearly sent ten swimmers to an early grave

May and June I rode on my bike,
in my lycra shorts I looked a sight.
After two months of cycling around,
scales showed I had lost one lousy pound.

July and August I walked everywhere,
was gasping and wheezing but I didn't care.
Walked up a big hill and nearly died,
so decided to roll down the other side.

September and October tried a skipping rope,
I went bright red and struggled to cope.
Could manage two minutes but if I tried more
I would collapse in a heap on the floor

November and December I called it a day,
reckon this weight is here to stay.
Hang on, I've just realised, oh bloody hell -
you're supposed to cut down on your food as well.

Lost World

The sun and moon struggle to shine,
grapes no longer grow on the vine.
Leaves on trees have turned to rust,
all grass has been replaced with dust.

The sea no longer ebbs and flows,
none of nature's beauty grows.
Birds don't sing or take to flight,
sky has become a ghostly white.

There's an eerie silence, everything's still,
this land's so sick it's terminally ill.
Today the earth broke down and cried,
gave up, surrendered, then slowly died.

Make Them Laugh

When the circus came to town
it had a vacancy for a clown.
But to become a member of staff
you had to make the animals laugh.

The first to apply drove the elephant mad,
kept telling jokes that were really bad.
So the elephant swung his trunk about,
hit the clown and knocked him out.

Next person to try was such a bore,
the poor old lion could take no more.
Lion roared with his mouth open wide,
clown got scared and ran off to hide.

The monkey wasn't impressed at all,
when someone else tried acting the fool.
Monkey bit him and slapped his head,
clown turned on his heels and quickly fled.

Another clown gave it a go.
Was he funny? Horse didn't think so.
Decided the best thing he could do
was kick him from here to Timbuktu.

The last to apply at the end of the day
soon had the animals laughing away.
He got the job and soon settled down,
now everyone loves Co-Co The Clown.

Mates

When Billy lent Barry a large sum of cash,
his so – called mate disappeared in a flash.
Down the pub his mates, Fred and Jim,
always wait for Billy to "get them in."

When he lent tools to his mate Jack,
he noticed that they never came back.
He lent his bike to a mate called Vince,
hasn't seen him or his bike since

His best mate, who he'd trust with his life,
borrowed his car and ran off with his wife.
All his friends took him for a fool -
that's why he became Billy no mates at all.

⌐~≈≈≈⌐

Merry-Go-Round II

The merry-go-round of life keeps spinning,
some people losing while others are winning.
Day after day it never stops turning,
the longer we ride the more we keep learning.

Sometimes a fast ride, other times slow,
just sit back, relax, and enjoy the show.
Each ride is different, some wild some tame,
as we all experience life's crazy game.

There will be nowhere to run or hide
when it's our turn to dismount this ride.
As we leave forever, new faces are found
to begin their ride on life's merry-go-round.

Music

When I used to visit Grandad at home,
he would turn on his old gramophone.
The records he played weren't that great,
thick old things called a seventy-eight.

My Dad thought he was the bees knees,
when he used to play his vinyl LPs.
His record player that cost a few quid
had a built in speaker and pull down lid.

Was sure I'd discovered the best thing yet
when I taped an LP onto a cassette.
On my stereo system it blared away,
a recordable C90 made by TDK.

Then as I grew older and greyer,
my son got himself a right fancy player.
You couldn't hear any crackle or hiss,
as he played music on compact disc.

Today my Grandson tried explaining to me
how to use iPod and MP3.
But I told him "You're wasting your time,
my new digital radio suits me just fine."

My Turn

Kelly's eye, number one,
the waiting game has begun.
Cup of tea, number three,
but this is no good to me.
Lucky for some, number seven,
is soon followed by legs eleven.
Number thirteen is unlucky and mean,
now it's coming of age, number eighteen.
Twenty one, the key to the door,
that's the one I've been waiting for.
It's my turn on the deli, what a relief.
I can finally get some ham and corned beef.

34

Next Door

For years she's lived in this little old house,
can't imagine living anywhere else.
She gets on with next door pretty well,
while others think they're "neighbours from hell."

The kids next door are not very quiet,
make so much noise, it sounds like a riot.
If they play tag or hide and seek,
they will scream and shout when they speak.

Sometimes she will hear a very loud roar,
then "bang-bang you're dead," when they play war.
Doesn't annoy her, it's no bother at all,
she's got used to living next door to a school.

Ninety Nine

I was a market trader doing just fine,
selling my T-shirts at £1.99.
But soon found out I didn't sell many,
when I tried asking two pound and a penny.

Managed to increase my sales once more,
by charging the same as I did before.
The easiest way to a profit, I've found,
is be one penny less than the nearest pound.

Used this idea on all of my stock;
it seemed to work, I sold a lot.
Found people were more likely to spend,
when my prices had ninety-nine at the end.

I started off with a market pitch,
worked hard and now I am very rich.
I turned that old market stall of mine
into a chain of shops, all called "Ninety-Nine."

Norman's Sweet Shop

There once was a shop, jam – packed with treats,
called "Norman's Good Old Fashioned Sweets."
Customers soon had a smile on their face
when they stepped inside this wonderful place.

He sold Black-Jacks, Bulls-Eyes and Acid Drops,
Gobstoppers, Love Hearts, Jelly Tots,
Pink Shrimps, Bon-Bons, White Chocolate Mice,
Tasty Sweet Tobacco that didn't look nice,

Dolly Mixtures, Refreshers, Tooty-Frooties as well,
Parma Violets, with their distinctive smell.
Traffic Light lollies that lasted for a long time,
Toasted Teacakes which tasted just divine.

Sherbet Fountains, Fruit Salads and many more,
but Norman didn't do well and sales were poor.
It's no wonder his business got into a fix,
as you don't make much profit on a 10p mix.

Old and Grey

Once grey hairs get on your head,
they multiply, then rapidly spread.
Before you know it, quick as a flash,
they're in your beard and moustache.

Then later they think you'll be impressed
if they start appearing on your chest.
Try kidding yourself that it looks cool,
as they stand out like wire wool.

Although you wish it wasn't so,
you start to spot them down below.
Use a mirror and you'll find
there's even some on your behind.

Guess it's Mother Nature's way
of telling us we're old and grey.
Well Mother Nature, two fingers to you,
I've bought some dye and turned mine blue.

One,Two,Three = A,B,C

9,6, 25,15,21,'18,5, 14,15,23, 18,5,1,4,9,14,7, 20,8,9,19,
3,15,14,7,18,1,20,21,12,1,20,9,15,14,19, 20,15, 25,15,21,
25,15,21, 13,21,19,20, 8,1,22,5, 23,15,18,11,5,4, 15,21,20,
20,8,1,20, 20,8,5, 20,9,20,12,5,'19, 20,8,5, 3,12,21,5,
23,8,25, 9,'22,5, 23,18,9,20,20,5,14, 9,14, 14,21,13,2,5,18,19,
9, 18,5,1,12,12,25, 4,15,14,'20, 11,14,15,23,
2,21,20, 9,20,'19, 19,15,13,5,20,8,9,14,7, 4,9,6,6,5,18,5,14,20,
19,15, 9, 7,1,22,5, 9,20, 1, 7,15,
2,21,20, 9, 17,21,9,3,11,12,25, 18,5,1,12,9,19,5,4,
3,15,14,22,5,18,20,9,14,7, 5,1,3,8, 12,9,14,5,
9,19, 2,15,18,9,14,7, 1,14,4, 20,1,11,5,19,
1, 2,12,15,15,4,25, 12,15,14,7, 20,9,13,5,
23,9,19,8, 9,'4, 14,5,22,5,18, 19,20,1,18,20,5,4,
14,15,23, 9, 11,14,15,23, 6,15,18, 19,21,18,5,
20,8,9,19, 9,19, 20,8,5, 12,1,19,20, 22,5,18,19,5,
9,'13, 14,15,20, 23,18,9,20,9,14,7, 14,15, 13,15,18,5.

39

Our Boss

Our boss at work is a funny old bloke,
drives a Rolls-Royce, but reckons he's broke.
Lives in a big house right by the sea,
but we don't even get free coffee or tea.

Ask for a rise and he'll go in a rage,
says he can only afford the minimum wage.
He dines in restaurants fit for the Queen
while we eat our sarnies in the canteen.

Even at Christmas, there's no festive cheer,
no bonus, no party, no presents, no beer.
And while he's on holiday cruising abroad,
a few days at home is all we can afford.

He tells us "work hard then maybe you'll be
respected and successful just like me."
But we all think he's a silly old fool,
and without us he'd have no business at all.

The workers whose hands get covered in blisters
all happen to be my brothers and sisters.
Having a famliy firm is a dead loss
when you've got a Dad like ours as your boss.

40

Over-Rated

He reckons that football is much over-rated,
men kicking some leather that's been inflated.
When it crosses a line between two sticks,
thousands of people are thrilled to bits.

When their team is rubbish and playing poor,
the fans still go mad if they manage to score.
Then they all curse at the match referee
if he makes a decision and they disagree.

Professional footballers want a fortune to play,
so each week at the turnstiles, supporters must pay.
The mega-rich players all drive flashy cars,
like drinking champagne in posh fancy bars.

For years football's been analysed and debated,
some people still think that it's over-rated.
Been to his first match, at age seventy-eight,
now changed his mind and thinks football's great.

41

Pen and Ink

My blue pen has a terrible knack
of running out, so I changed to black.
I had swapped but I didn't know,
this black pen was getting low.
I'm now using a red rollerball,
already it will not write at all.
I've switched to a biro with navy ink -
this one's working alright I think.
Spoke too soon, that pen's now dead,
in future I'm going to write in lead.
This pencil is now my best mate,
but I think the lead's about to break.

◆━═━◆

Popped in the Chemist

Popped in the chemist because she felt down,
man behind the counter said "Why the frown?
Whatever your problem I'm pretty sure
that I'll be able to find you a cure.

We've got lotions, potions, tablets and pills,
to make you feel better and fix any ills.
Bandages and plasters to put on your skin,
there's even a drink that helps you to slim.

We sell fancy ointment for rashes and spots,
bottles of tonic for the back-door trots.
Soothing cream for very stiff necks,
packets of condoms to enjoy safe sex."

When she told him why she was feeling blue,
he said "I'm sorry, but we can't help you.
I've looked high and low, torn this shop apart -
but we've nothing at all for a broken heart."

43

Quiz Night

In a sleepy village there is an old inn,
on quiz night the farmers all try to win.
It's expensive to enter, but once everyone's paid,
first prize is a weekend, with the barmaid.

One night the winner was old farmer Giles,
who is eighty and suffers with painful piles.
The barmaid turned white when he took her hand
and whispered to her what he had planned.

Saturday morning he told her, "Now I've got you,
we can start on my list of things to do -
First job's clean the cow shed, it stinks like hell,
then the old pig-sty needs looking at as well."

They fed the poultry and hosed down the yard,
she was enjoying herself, even though it was hard.
When that was all done they rounded up sheep.
That night in the spare room she soon fell asleep.

She told him on Sunday, this weekend's been fun,
I'm covered in muck, but we got a lot done.
Monday old farmer Giles told all his friends
"That barmaids great. She likes dirty weekends."

44

Rescued

She was in the crowd walking along,
stopped for five minutes then they were gone.
Couldn't believe that in no time at all,
she was now alone and felt a right fool.

By not keeping up, she learnt to her cost,
just how quickly you can become lost.
Walked for ages 'til her feet were sore,
thought she'd be OK, but now she's not sure.

Then in the distance she happened to see,
a man who was shouting "Those lost follow me."
She was totally lost so she had no choice,
and followed the man with the booming voice.

He said "Getting lost is not much fun,
but you're not the first and it's easily done.
You will be surprised how many ways,
there is to get lost in this garden maze."

Rock 'N' Roll

Goodness gracious, bless my soul,
the radio's playing rock 'n' roll.
Now I'm jiving with my girl Molly
to Bill Haley and Buddy Holly.

Little Richard, Gene Vincent, Fats Domino
they're playing all the songs we know.
Eddie Cochran, Del Shannon, Chubby Checker,
the music keeps getting better and better.

We both love to hear all the old hits,
then shuffle around on our walking sticks.
Tonight's rock 'n' roll hour has been bliss,
gave two old farts chance to reminisce.

Rubbish Rashers

Billy Bacon felt scared as he lay in the packet,
said to his mate, "Don't think I can hack it.
We're the last two slices and I'm feeling ill,
it looks like we're going under the grill."

His friend said "Buck up and act like a man,
at least we're not heading for the frying pan.
In the frying pan oil it's easy to drown,
but under the grill we turn nice and brown."

They stayed together as they went in the bread,
then got covered in sauce, all runny and red.
Billy Bacon whispered to his old friend
"I think our journey is nearing its end."

Entering the mouth, Billy heard a shout.
A voice said "Oh no, my tooth's fallen out."
As they got thrown away, they started to grin,
then both settled down in the kitchen bin.

Rum and Ribena

Was in my local having a beer,
when the landlord whispered in my ear,
"See that old dear, there's no one meaner,
once she's knocked back the rum and Ribena."

Then he told me the story of Gran
who could be as gentle as a lamb,
other times she would act the fool
and be as stubborn as a mule.

Always first out the starting blocks
because she is as sly as a fox.
They say her eyesight isn't all that,
rumour has it she's as blind as a bat.

Ask for advice and she'll advise you well,
with age she's become as wise as an owl.
But once in a while just for a dare,
she will act like a mad march hare.

If she uses her charm you will be smitten,
sometimes she can be as cute as a kitten.
Has managed to overcome all life's knocks,
she's as brave as a lion and as strong as an ox.

Her favourite tipple is rum and Ribena.
She drinks like a fish, laughs like a hyena.
But she can't handle her drink at all,
when drunk she turns into a right animal.

School Reunion

At the school reunion Mary looked around
and was surprised at what she found.
She'd got dressed up, had her hair done,
but by the look of things she's the only one.

Bike shed Sheila's still a hit with the lads,
now has six kids with six different dads.
Posh rich Penny who was clever but lippy
lives in a bus and is now a hippy.

The big butch girl named Diane
now calls herself Dave and looks like a man.
Pauline the punk who scared everyone
found religion and is now a nun.

Luscious Linda, the good looking lass,
now has saggy boobs and a big fat ass.
But Amanda with the attitude
is still obnoxious, nasty and rude.

Mary hoped this reunion would be a blast,
meeting up with old faces from the past.
Thank God I'm retired she now thought,
as she met the girls that she once taught.

Shot Down

One hundred pilots
went flying off to war,
they all got shot down
so the Air Force sent some more.

Nine hundred seamen
went sailing off to war,
they all got shot down
so the Navy sent some more.

Four thousand soldiers
went marching off to war,
they all got shot down
so the Army sent some more.

All the Armed Forces
tried to settle a score,
five thousand lives were lost
so the Government sent some more.

Now the war is over,
it's come to an end.
Everybody's been shot down,
there's no one left to send.

Something to Do

Walked out of the kitchen with her cup of tea,
went into the lounge, turned on the TV.
Phoned a friend and yakked away,
then finished the ironing left from yesterday.

Made herself a sandwich, cheese and onion,
rubbed ointment on her painful bunion.
Read some of her book, a Mills and Boon,
went round with the duster in the front room.

Did some of her jigsaw that's taken an age,
then fed the budgie and cleaned his cage.
Ran some water for a nice hot bath,
remembered a joke that made her laugh.

Put a few towels in the washing machine,
tried doing a crossword in her magazine.
She's agoraphobic, spends the whole day through
staying indoors finding something to do.

Spots

There once was a boy called Rodney Rose,
who had a small spot on the end of his nose.
In the mirror each morning he squeezed it with vigour,
and the spot on his nose grew bigger and bigger.

Wouldn't leave it alone, he kept squeezing it,
so his small spot turned into a zit.
Then later Rodney had even more trouble,
when it started to look like a big white bubble.

In the bathroom he moaned and he cursed,
then squeezed real hard but it never burst.
Said to himself "hope this does the trick",
as he stabbed the spot with a sharp toothpick.

The spot exploded and made him scream,
pus began pouring out like soft ice-cream.
Now at last his big spot is no more,
but it's left his nose all tender and sore.

If a small spot appears on the end of your nose,
just remember what happened to Rodney Rose.
Or ignore this story and act like a man,
and squeeze the bugger as hard as you can.

Sunday Roast

My age is showing, I'm getting old,
losing my teeth, notice the cold.
Often don't hear what people say,
keep nodding off during the day.

Becoming unstable on my feet,
can't walk far before I'm beat.
Now my eyesight is very poor,
I'm not so confident any more.

My memory's gone, it's totally shot,
I need to empty my bladder a lot.
I'm going downhill pretty fast,
reckon this year might be my last.

I find the simplest tasks are a slog,
now that I'm a tired old dog.
But when I sniff that roast dinner smell,
I can still bark and wag my tail.

Tablets

My tablets are great, they keep me alive,
so each week I'm taking one hundred and five.
If I didn't have them, don't know what I'd do,
probably stop breathing and then turn blue.

Take one each morning, knowing full well,
if I don't my chest will burn like hell.
My next tablet plays a major part,
makes sure there's a steady beat to my heart.

Two more tablets this morning, then that's my lot,
they help with the diabetes I've got.
That's the morning tablets out of the way,
then I've got two more to take at midday.

When it's near 5pm I know for sure,
with my tea it's time for some more.
Another three tablets, I swallow them quick,
they stop my blood from getting too thick.

There's still more to take, oh me, oh my,
next one's because my cholesterol's too high.
My sugar levels make my doctor frown,
so swallow two tablets and hope it comes down.

It's getting late, time to rest my head,
a few more tablets then I'm off to bed.
One more for cholesterol, two for the pain,
then tomorrow I'll take them all over again.

Takeaway

Big Bill would often get in a mood
if he couldn't have his favourite junk food.
His mates all told him a takeaway
would be the cause of his death one day.

He loved donor kebabs with chilli sauce,
had the biggest one they did, of course.
Thought fish and chips were so nice,
he always ordered the same meal twice.

Could eat four burgers no trouble at all,
he just kept eating and never got full.
Loved his pizza, thought curries were great,
you would never believe how much he ate.

A driver out delivering a chinese meal
accidentally ran down and killed poor Bill.
Now his friends swear it's true when they say
Big Bill was killed by a takeaway.

Teetotal

When I get drunk on Malibu,
I fall asleep and dream of you.
But when I have too much rum,
I have nightmares about your mum.

If I knock back lots of gin,
in my dreams I'm fit and slim.
And if I drink Bacardi and coke,
I dream that I'm a wealthy bloke.

After I've had a lot of whisky,
I'll dream I'm doing something risky.
When I down a nice cool beer,
I dream I'm brave and have no fear.

Then each time I drink champagne,
I dream I'm twenty-one again.
And if I drink a lot of Port,
I dream I'm healthy and good at sport.

I've found out if I only drink tea,
I sleep soundly and dream – free.
So now most nights it's tea I'm pouring,
but compared to booze, it ain't half boring.

◄━━━━━►

The End

When my life is over
and I am dead and gone,
cry for me if you want to,
but don't mourn for too long.

Announce my death in the paper,
write a heartfelt verse.
Then I'll take my final journey,
with horses pulling my hearse.

My funeral's not a fund-raiser,
there'll be no "Donations to".
Cover my coffin in flowers,
anything in full bloom will do.

Parting always brings sorrow,
there's no happy ever after.
So remember the good times,
the fun, and all the laughter.

Never believed in the following:
the afterlife, heaven or hell.
When I die that is the end -
Goodbye. So long. Farewell.

Thingy

I'm stood here with tears in my eyes,
I've got my thingy caught in my flies.
My Dad's told me, "Stand still nipper,
and I'll see if I can move your zipper."

I said "No" and shook my head,
when Mum said "Shall I do it instead?"
By now my thingy was turning blue,
but some things your Mum, just shouldn't do.

Braced myself as Dad had a go
at freeing my thingy from down below.
He tugged my zip, I gave a shout,
now my thingy's free and swinging about.

One week later my thingy's still sore,
and I don't like using my zip anymore.
But I'll be alright, my Mum's just said
I can have some trousers with buttons instead.

⟨ ˜˜ ⟩

Town and Country

On the school run, parked in the street,
you will always see Range Rovers and Jeeps.
Been thinking about it but still I'm unsure
why town people need a 4x4.

Outside the shops they all drive around
until a large space has been found.
Ten minutes later they've got red faces,
and have used up two parking spaces.

Drive to the supermarket and back,
but never off road, or down a track.
On the streets you see more and more,
haven't a clue what they need them for.

Can't see counrty folk deciding one day
a small car is perfect for carrying hay.
And a farmer would expect to get flak
if on muddy fields he drove a hatchback.

You would think everyone who lives in a town,
would just use a car for getting around.
Wonder why some people think that it's neat
to drive 4x4s, Range Rovers and Jeeps.

Upset Eyes

I cry at the truth,
I cry at the lies,
I keep crying tears
from these upset eyes.

I cry when it's dark,
I cry when it's light,
I cry when I'm wrong,
I cry when I'm right.

I cry when it's hot,
I cry when it's cold,
I cry when I'm asked,
I cry when I'm told.

I cry when it's cloudy,
I cry when it's fine,
I cry for no reason,
I cry all the time.

I'm not very tough,
I'm soft as a pillow,
the other trees call me
the sad Weeping Willow.

Valerie

He picked up his wife's golden locket,
then placed it gently in his trouser pocket.
Inside the locket's a photo of Valerie,
to remind him of how she used to be.

She wasn't exactly a good looking girl,
bald as a coot, except for one curl.
Her eyes are the colour of a blood red rose,
and both point inwards towards her nose.

Her nose looks funny and out of place,
like an old mushroom stuck on her face.
She has also got two big massive cheeks,
looks like she's been storing food up for weeks.

The few teeth she has are yellow and brown,
her ears appear to be on upside down.
She has weird shaped lips and a lopsided grin,
a giant hairy mole on the end of her chin.

He looked at her photo and thouht "what a cutie",
reckoned his Valerie was a real beauty.
Rang the church bells the day his wife died,
then Quasimodo broke down and cried.

61

Village Gossips

At the village surgery the new young GP
was going out with sexy Marie.
Wherever they went she loved to flirt,
which left him upset and feeling hurt.

It didn't take long for him to discover,
that Marie was unfaithful and had a lover.
She was seeing the vicar, Mr Apple,
who she met in secret, inside the chapel.

He confronted Marie, said "How could you?
And with the vicar, that's it we're through."
The GP went home and started to pack,
then left the village and never came back.

The villagers thought that Marie was a cow,
seeing Reverend Apple each day as well.
Now in the village the gossips all say
an Apple a day keeps the doctor away.

Wendy Wannabe

A girl called Wendy Wannabe
thought it would be cool
to be rich and famous,
but she had no talent at all.

Managed to get on the TV,
in a cheap "Big Brother type show."
Acted like she was famous,
but was the first to go.

Had a go at modelling,
posed without her bra.
Acted like she was famous,
but never became a star.

She married a top football player,
who is brilliant with a ball.
Wendy Wannabe's now rich and famous,
but still has no talent at all.

What's for Tea

Oh laudy, oh daudy, oh deary me,
don't know what to cook for our tea.
Keep it simple like bangers and mash,
or get out the wok and do something flash.

Liver and bacon, perhaps shepherd's pie,
something frozen made by Birds Eye.
Now I wish I had gone to the shops,
and bought a couple of lovely lamb chops.

Could make a hotpot or maybe a stew,
cauliflower cheese is quite easy to do.
Trying to make a decision has got on my tits,
so I'm off up the road for some fish and chips.

❧

Why

I was dreaming that I could fly,
then landed on a cloud in the sky.
Cloud said to me "I don't mean to pry,
but what are you doing up this high?"

I told the cloud a little white lie,
said that I was a government spy.
He reckoned my humour was very dry,
then gave a smile and winked his eye.

I heard my alarm clock, so said goodbye,
then woke up in bed and let out a sigh.
Now if I can't sleep I know what to try;
just think of words that rhyme with why.

Wishing-Well

I made a wish at the wishing-well,
then I promised not to tell.
I waited for a week or two,
the wish I made never came true.
Went to the well – told it I was mad,
asked for a bike, got a saddle bag.
A voice from the well said "In my defence,
what did you expect, for ten lousy pence?"

Wonderful Water

There's a coach driver as old as the hills,
who never needs any tablets or pills.
He may look old but he's fit and strong,
you'll find out why if you read on.

All the pensioners have gathered once more,
for their annual mystery coach tour.
Driver sets off and they give a cheer,
always go to the same place, year after year.

When they arrive at the back of beyond,
they'll take the path next to the pond.
Everyone will walk for a mile or two,
they know it's worth it if they do.

Then just before the big oak trees
is the sign saying: "This way please."
After they've paid the man in the booth,
they can enter the fountain of youth.

The fountain of youth takes away all pain,
that's why they revisit again and again.
Drinking the water makes them stronger,
and helps them live for a lot longer.

The old coach driver whose name is Ron,
makes the fountain of youth look like a con.
He's all hunched up, wrinkly and bald,
but swears he's now five hundred years old.

X Marks the Spot

In the amusement arcade on the fruit machine,
he kept hitting the button, he was very keen.
But an hour later he had to give in,
his pockets were empty and he didn't win.

Tried playing poker, he bet more and more,
thought these are the winning cards for sure.
Felt certain that he would win a few grand,
then he got beaten by a much better hand.

He went along to the local racecourse,
picked himself out a fine looking horse.
Bet a load of money, then got the hump,
his horse pulled up at the very first jump.

The gambler sat on his old kitchen stool,
then filled in a form for Spot the Ball.
He thought "for years I've been having a bet,
this is the only thing I haven't tried yet."

Just been told that he's won the jackpot,
can't believe the size of the cheque he's got.
The only time he's bet and not lost
is when he gambled on a little black cross.

68

Yesterday

Night will soon come and find us,
like it did the day before.
Then by the break of dawn,
yesterday wll be no more.

Morning has started appearing,
today looks pleasant and fine.
It passes by far too quickly,
is gone in such a short time.

Each new day never lasts forever,
but no matter come what may,
none of us can stop tomorrow,
or return back to yesterday.

69

Yum-Yum

I first noticed Yum-Yum in a glossy magazine,
was the best looking Thai bride I have ever seen.
Thought I had been ripped off, she took ages to come,
then today she turned up, my lovely Yum-Yum.

She is a real stunner, with silky jet black hair,
doesn't speak any English, but I don't really care.
Feeling very happy now that she is mine,
I'm sure that me and Yum-Yum will get along just fine.

Took things very slowly, in bed on our first night,
was nervous and excited, hoped it would be alright.
I was huffing and puffing then I felt elated,
she now looked even better, blown up and inflated.

Zipping Past

There was a young author, his books always sold,
people loved to read all the tales that he told.
He would tell stories that would leave you aghast,
and the minutes and hours keep on zipping past.

The middle – aged author still writes every day,
he's in demand so carries on typing away.
Can't believe that his novels are selling so fast,
and the months and years keep on zipping past.

The old author was lying on his death bed,
said "I hope when I'm gone my books are still read.
This book I've just written will be my last,
it's appropriately called, *Life Keeps Zipping Past*."